MW01098649

Land of Liberty

Vermont

by Barbara Knox

Consultant:
Dr. Paul Searls
Professor of History
University of Vermont

Capstone
press
Mankato, Minnesota

Capstone Press
151 Good Counsel Drive • P.O. Box 669 • Mankato, Minnesota 56002
http://www.capstone-press.com

Library of Congress Cataloging-in-Publication Data
Knox, Barbara.
  Vermont / by Barbara Knox.
    p. cm.—(Land of liberty)
  Includes bibliographical references and index.
  Contents: About Vermont—Land, climate, and wildlife—History of
Vermont—Government and politics—Economy and resources—People and
culture—Almanac.
  ISBN 0-7368-2201-1 (hardcover)
  1. Vermont—Juvenile literature. [1. Vermont.] I. Title. II. Series.
F49.3.K58 2004
974.3—dc21   2002155000

Summary: An introduction to the geography, history, government, politics,
economy, resources, people, and culture of Vermont, including maps, charts,
and a recipe.

Editorial Credits
Angela Kaelberer, editor; Jennifer Schonborn, series designer; Molly Nei,
    book designer; Enoch Peterson, illustrator; Heather Atkinson and Jo Miller,
    photo researchers; Eric Kudalis, product planning editor

Photo Credits
Cover images: Farmstead near Pomfret, Corbis/Peter Finger; Mount Mansfield, Unicorn
Stock Photos/Andre Jenny

AP/Wide World Photos/Toby Talbot, 31; Bruce Coleman Inc., 17, Phil Degginger, 56;
Capstone Press/Gary Sundermeyer, 54; Comstock, 1; Corbis, 28, Jason Furnari, 38; Getty
Images/Hulton Archive, 18, 20–21, 27, 36; Houserstock/Dave G. Houser, 46, Michael J.
Pettypool, 53; Index Stock Imagery/Dennis Curran, 41, 45; North Wind Picture Archives,
22, 24, 58; One Mile Up Inc., 55 (both); Pat & Chuck Blackley, 42–43; Tom Till, 8;
Unicorn Stock Photos/A. Gurmankin, 4; Andre Jenny, 12–13, 32, 50–51, 63; Marshall
Prescott, 14; U.S. Postal Service, 59; Visuals Unlimited/Maslowski, 57

Artistic Effects
Corbis, Digital Vision, PhotoDisc

1 2 3 4 5 6 08 07 06 05 04 03

Table of Contents

Thick forests cover Vermont's Green Mountain range.

Chapter 1

About Vermont

The Green Mountains stretch through the middle of Vermont from north to south. Forests of evergreen, birch, and maple trees cover the Green Mountains. The color of the thick forests gives the range its name.

The Green Mountains are part of the Appalachian range. The Appalachians begin in the southeastern United States and extend north into Canada.

The Green Mountains are a popular year-round vacation area. In fall, tourists travel to Vermont to see the trees' colorful leaves. Skiers come to the area's resorts in winter. In summer, hikers travel the Long Trail, the oldest long-distance hiking path in the United States. The Long Trail is 270 miles

(435 kilometers) long. It spans the entire length of Vermont as it runs along the Green Mountains.

Green Mountain State

In the early 1600s, French explorers came to present-day Vermont. The explorers called the Green Mountains "les verts monts," which means "the green mountains." The state's name comes from these French words. Today, Vermont is known as the Green Mountain State.

Vermont is one of the smallest states, but it is the second largest of the six New England states. Only Maine is larger.

Vermont's neighbors include three states and a Canadian province. New York borders Vermont on the west, and Massachusetts lies to the south. The Connecticut River separates Vermont from New Hampshire to the east. The Canadian province of Quebec is north of Vermont.

Vermont Cities

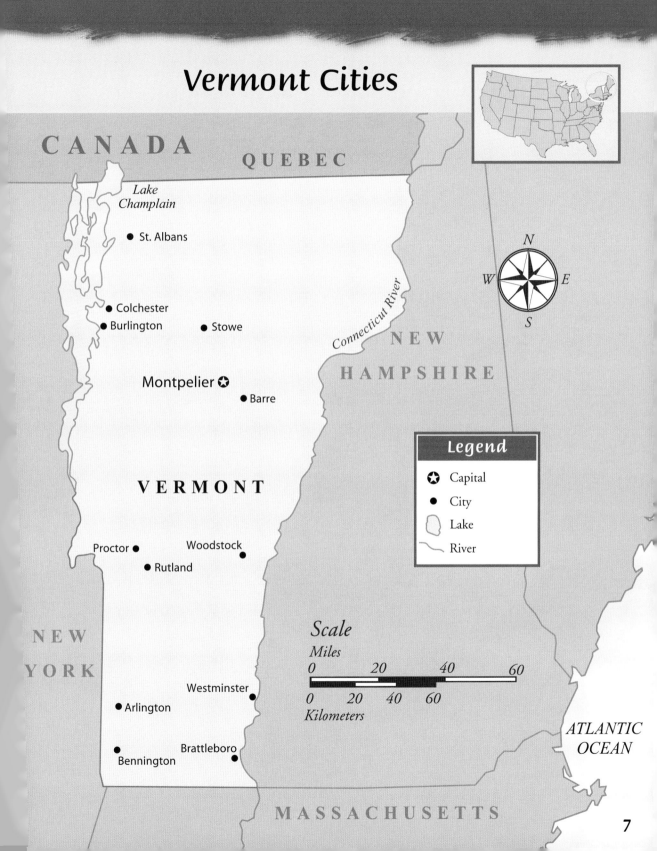

CANADA

QUEBEC

Lake Champlain

• St. Albans

Connecticut River

NEW HAMPSHIRE

N
W   E
S

• Colchester
• Burlington   • Stowe

Montpelier ✪
• Barre

VERMONT

NEW YORK

Proctor •   Woodstock •
• Rutland

Legend

✪ Capital
• City
⬭ Lake
〜 River

Westminster •

• Arlington

Scale
Miles
0   20   40   60

0   20   40   60
Kilometers

Brattleboro •
Bennington •

ATLANTIC OCEAN

MASSACHUSETTS

Small plants called lichen cover white quartz rocks on Mount Mansfield, Vermont's highest point.

Chapter 2

Land, Climate, and Wildlife

Vermont's land is marked by mountains and rolling hills. Almost none of the state is flat.

Vermont can be divided into six main regions. These regions are the Green Mountains, the Taconic Mountains, the Valley of Vermont, the Piedmont, the Northeast Highlands, and the Champlain Valley.

Green Mountains

The Green Mountains are smaller than many mountain ranges. Most of the range's peaks are about 2,000 feet (600 meters) high. A few peaks are more than 4,000 feet (1,200 meters) high.

The state's highest point is in the Green Mountains. Mount Mansfield is 4,393 feet (1,339 meters) above sea level. From the east, the mountain looks like the side of a person's face. The mountain has five peaks. The peaks are called the Adam's Apple, the Chin, the Lips, the Nose, and the Forehead. The Chin is the mountain's highest point.

Taconic Mountains

The Taconic Mountains are in southwestern Vermont. The highest peak in the range is Mount Equinox, which is 3,816 feet (1,163 meters) high.

The rock in the Taconic range is sedimentary. It formed from layers of rock, sand, and soil. Most of Vermont's slate and marble quarries are located in this range.

The Valley of Vermont

The Valley of Vermont lies between the Taconic Mountains and the Green Mountains. The valley is the smallest of the state's regions. It stretches from west-central Vermont to just north of the Massachusetts border.

The longest river within Vermont winds through the valley. Otter Creek flows 100 miles (160 kilometers) until it reaches Lake Champlain.

Vermont's Land Features

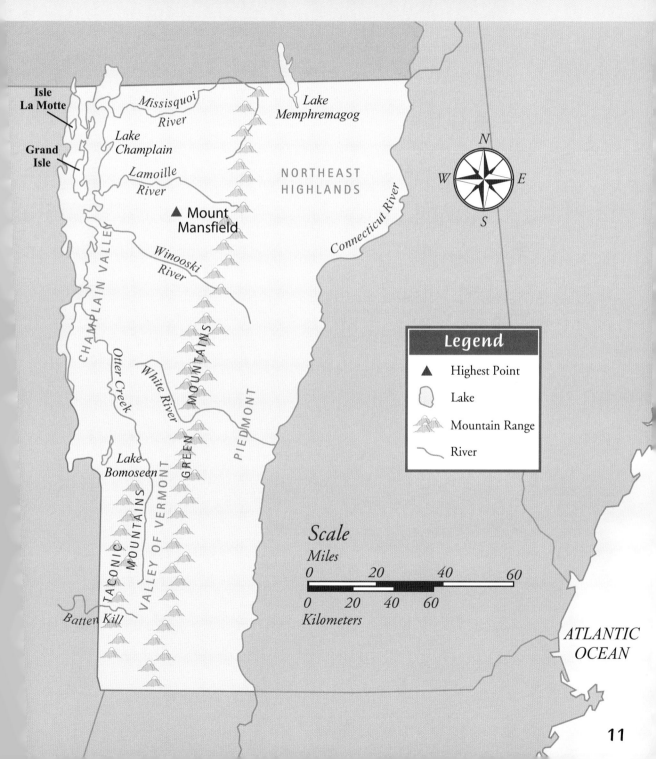

Isle
La Motte

Grand
Isle

Missisquoi
River

Lake
Champlain

Lamoille
River

Lake
Memphremagog

NORTHEAST
HIGHLANDS

Connecticut River

▲ Mount
Mansfield

CHAMPLAIN VALLEY

Winooski
River

Otter Creek

White River

GREEN MOUNTAINS

PIEDMONT

Lake
Bomoseen

TACONIC MOUNTAINS

VALLEY OF VERMONT

Batten Kill

N
W   E
S

Legend

▲ Highest Point

⬭ Lake

⛰ Mountain Range

〜 River

Scale

Miles

0   20   40   60

0   20   40   60

Kilometers

ATLANTIC
OCEAN

Piedmont

The Piedmont is Vermont's largest region. The word "piedmont" means "at the foot of the mountain." The Piedmont lies east of the Green Mountains and covers most of eastern Vermont.

Two smaller regions are within the Piedmont. The rich soil of the Connecticut River Valley is in the eastern part of the region. There, farmers grow apples and raise sheep and dairy cattle. In the west, the Granite Hills are home to the world's largest granite quarries.

Northeast Highlands

The Northeast Highlands region in northeast Vermont is sometimes called the Northeast Kingdom or the White Mountains region. The Connecticut River separates the Northeast Highlands from New Hampshire's White Mountains.

The Northeast Highlands is a hilly area with poor, rocky soil. Few people live there. In winter, the region has some of the coldest temperatures in the state. The area also includes some of the state's largest swamps and bogs.

Forests and rolling hills cover the land near Peacham in the Northeast Highlands.

Champlain Valley

The Champlain Valley is bordered by Lake Champlain to the west, the Green Mountains to the east, and the Taconic Mountains to the south. The region is also called the Vermont Lowlands.

The Green Mountains protect the Champlain Valley from extremes in temperature. The mild climate and rich clay soil make the valley an important farming region.

Rivers and Lakes

Most of Vermont's rivers flow through the Green Mountains and drain into either Lake Champlain in the west or the

About 75 percent of Lake Champlain is in northwestern Vermont. The rest of the lake is in New York and Canada.

Connecticut River in the east. Besides Otter Creek, major rivers in Vermont include the Batten Kill, White, Lamoille, Missisquoi, and Winooski.

Two lakes form part of the state's boundaries. Lake Memphremagog (mem-fruh-MAY-gawg) forms part of Vermont's northern border with Canada. About 25 percent of the lake lies within Vermont. Lake Champlain is the sixth largest freshwater lake in the United States. It covers 430 square miles (1,114 square kilometers). Vermont shares the lake with New York and Quebec. Many of Lake Champlain's large islands are part of Vermont. These islands include Grand Isle and Isle La Motte.

About 400 smaller lakes are found in Vermont. Lake Bomoseen is the largest lake that lies entirely within the state. It covers 4 square miles (10 square kilometers). The Piedmont contains many lakes formed by ice sheets called glaciers. These lakes include Lake Willoughby and Crystal Lake.

Climate

Vermont has a cool climate throughout the year. The average summer temperature is 65 degrees Fahrenheit (18 degrees Celsius). Vermont winters are cold and snowy. In winter, the average high temperature is 18 degrees Fahrenheit (minus 8 degrees Celsius).

Vermont receives an average of 40 inches (102 centimeters) of precipitation each year. During summer, the north and west receive more rain than the rest of the state. Almost all of Vermont receives heavy snowfall in winter. Some mountain areas receive as much as 125 inches (318 centimeters) of snow cach winter. Blizzards often strike Vermont during winter. Spring floods often result from the heavy snowfall.

Plants and Wildlife

Forests once covered most of Vermont, but early settlers cut down most of these trees to build farms and towns. By the late 1800s, forests covered only about 20 percent of the state.

In the early 1900s, Vermont began a program to reforest the state. By 2000, forests again covered more than 75 percent of Vermont. About 350,000 acres (142,000 hectares) of forested mountain land in southern Vermont is set aside as the Green Mountain National Forest. The forest includes more than 500 miles (805 kilometers) of hiking trails.

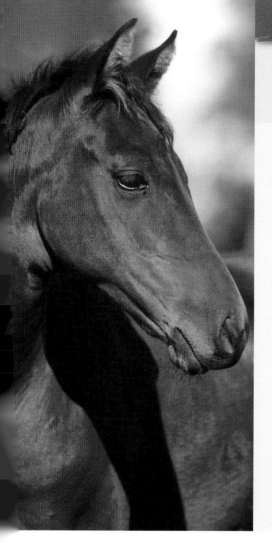

Morgan Horse

The Morgan horse breed began in Vermont. In 1789, Randolph schoolteacher Justin Morgan received a young stallion in payment of a debt. Morgan named the colt Figure.

Figure grew into a sturdy, fast horse with a gentle nature. Figure passed his good features to his many colts. People began calling Figure and his colts "Morgan" horses.

Today, Morgans are prized for their beauty, strength, and gentleness. Vermont named the Morgan horse its state animal in 1961.

Vermont's mountains, forests, and wetlands provide homes for many animals and birds. Mink, raccoon, and beaver hunt near the state's lakes and rivers. Ospreys, great blue herons, belted kingfishers, and other large birds also live near the water. Moose, white-tailed deer, and black bears make their homes in Vermont's forests.

French explorer Samuel de Champlain reached present-day Vermont in 1609.

Chapter 3

History of Vermont

Historians believe Paleo-Indians were living in what is now Vermont as early as 10,000 B.C. At that time, much of the area was covered by a saltwater sea connected to the Atlantic Ocean.

By A.D. 1000, two groups of native peoples lived in the region. Abenaki Indians built small villages near rivers in the Champlain and Connecticut River Valleys. The Mahican people lived in southwestern Vermont.

In 1609, French explorer Samuel de Champlain sailed through what is now Lake Champlain. Champlain claimed the region for France.

In 1724, English colonists from Massachusetts built Fort Dummer near present-day Brattleboro. The fort was the first permanent European settlement in Vermont.

The arrival of the Europeans hurt the Abenaki. Many Abenaki died from smallpox and other diseases brought by the Europeans.

Early Settlement

For much of the 1700s, different groups fought over ownership of Vermont. The French controlled the region until the mid-1700s. In 1749, British Governor Benning Wentworth of New Hampshire began giving Vermont land to

people in Connecticut and New Hampshire. These pieces of land were called "New Hampshire Grants."

In 1754, the French and Indian War (1754–1763) began between the British and the French. The surviving Abenaki Indians joined with the French to fight the British. The Treaty of Paris ended the French and Indian War and gave the New Hampshire Grants to Great Britain. After the war ended, many settlers moved to the New Hampshire Grants.

British and French soldiers fought the French and Indian War. After the war, Great Britain gained control of the New Hampshire Grants.

"I am as determined to preserve the independence of Vermont as Congress is that of the Union; and rather than fail, I will retire with my hardy Green Mountain Boys into the caverns of the mountains and make war on all mankind."
—Ethan Allen, leader of the Green Mountain Boys

Green Mountain Boys

In 1764, British King George III decided that the New Hampshire Grants should be part of New York. New Yorkers began to move to the New Hampshire Grants. The settlers did not want to lose their land to New Yorkers.

About 1770, settler Ethan Allen organized the Green Mountain Boys. This group wanted to force the New Yorkers to leave the western New Hampshire Grants. Allen led the group in sneak attacks on New Yorkers in both the New Hampshire Grants and the New York colony. The Green Mountain Boys drove many New Yorkers from the region.

In 1775, the Revolutionary War (1775–1783) began between the American colonies and Great Britain. Nearly all of the Green Mountain Boys chose to support American independence. On May 10, 1775, the Green Mountain Boys captured British Fort Ticonderoga. The fort was on Lake Champlain in northern New York.

Many former Green Mountain Boys fought for the Americans in the Battle of Bennington. In June 1777, British General John Burgoyne and his troops left Montreal, Canada.

They traveled by boat on Lake Champlain to New York. In August, Burgoyne and his troops stopped near Bennington in present-day Vermont. The soldiers tried to steal supplies from American storehouses there. On August 16, American soldiers attacked Burgoyne's soldiers just across the New York border. The Americans killed about 200 British troops and captured 700 more. Burgoyne surrendered about two months later.

An Independent Republic

New Yorkers still wanted the New Hampshire Grants to be part of their colony. In January 1777, settlers from the New Hampshire Grants met in Westminster. They declared their independence from New York and called their republic

In May 1775, Ethan Allen and the Green Mountain Boys captured Fort Ticonderoga during a surprise attack. The British gave up the fort without a fight.

New Connecticut. In June, the republic's leaders met again. They changed the republic's name to the Free and Independent State of Vermont. In July, Vermonters adopted their first constitution.

After defeating Great Britain, the 13 colonies became the United States of America. New York and New Hampshire each wanted Vermont to be part of their state, but Vermont remained independent. In 1790, Vermont paid New York $30,000 for land granted to Vermont settlers nearly 30 years earlier. That payment settled New York's claim on Vermont.

In 1791, Vermont was finally allowed to join the United States. Vermont became the 14th state on March 4, 1791.

During the 1800s, Vermont was a top producer of sheep.

War of 1812

In the early 1800s, U.S. leaders were upset with the British Navy. British ships often stopped U.S. ships to search for British sailors on board. They sometimes captured American sailors. In 1812, the United States again declared war on Great Britain.

Most Vermonters stayed out of the War of 1812 (1812–1814) as much as possible. Vermont and the rest of the New England states depended a great deal on trade with the British colony of Canada. Some Vermonters continued to trade with Canadian companies.

In August 1813, British ships attacked the town of Burlington from Lake Champlain. U.S. ships drove the British from the lake in September 1814. In December 1814, the Treaty of Ghent ended the war.

Transportation and Settlement

After the war, improved transportation systems brought more settlers to Vermont. In 1823, the Champlain Canal connected Lake Champlain to the Hudson River. Canals helped the Connecticut River become a major water route as well. Between 1800 and 1830, Vermont's population nearly doubled.

Many of the settlers raised sheep for both meat and wool. By 1840, about 1.6 million sheep grazed in Vermont's pastures.

Civil War

Slavery was a major issue for the United States in the 1800s. In 1777, the Free and Independent State of Vermont had outlawed slavery before any of the states did. Northern states later passed similar laws, but slavery remained legal in the South.

In 1860 and 1861, 11 Southern states left the Union to form the Confederate States of America. This action led to the Civil War (1861–1865).

Although no Civil War battles were fought in Vermont, the state was among the first to offer soldiers to the Union Army. About 35,000 Vermont men helped the Union win the war.

Economic Growth

By the mid-1800s, railroads brought more economic growth to Vermont. Small villages along the route became busy cities. Railroads delivered Vermont stone to builders across the country. Refrigerated railcars carried Vermont milk, cheese, and butter to Boston, Massachusetts, and other large cities.

The railroad also helped Vermont's manufacturing industry grow. Factories in Springfield and Windsor made machine tools, parts, and other metal goods. Burlington factories

Chester Arthur

Chester Arthur served as the nation's 21st president. Arthur was born October 5, 1829, in Fairfield. In 1880, he was elected vice president under James Garfield. In 1881, Garfield died in office, and Arthur became president. In 1883, Arthur signed the Civil Service Act. This law created a testing system used to hire government workers. Arthur did not run for president in 1884 because of illness. He died November 18, 1886.

turned the state's trees into furniture, pulp, and paper. Textile mill workers in Burlington wove cotton and wool into cloth.

Hard Times and War

Vermont's population began to drop in the 1870s. Some farmers moved to western states and territories, where land was cheap. Other people left Vermont for jobs in Boston and other large eastern cities. Small towns and farms disappeared as people moved away.

In 1917, the United States entered World War I (1914–1918). About 14,000 Vermonters served in the war.

The Flood of 1927 was Vermont's worst natural disaster. The floodwaters left many of Montpelier's buildings and streets in ruins.

A Deadly Disaster

In 1927, New England was hit with a major flood. The worst flooding occurred in Vermont. During October 1927, the state received above-average rainfall. The land was soaked. On November 2, 3, and 4, rain fell steadily across most of the state. Between 6 and 9 inches (15 and 23 centimeters) of rain

"As if drunk with its new-found power, [the river] staggered and roared its crooked way down the valley, ripping out trees, tearing away houses, barns, bridges, and gathering livestock and even human beings into its awful arms until spent with its Herculean effort, it passed mutteringly out into Lake Champlain."

—*R. E. Atwood,* Stories and Pictures of the Vermont Flood, November 2 and 3, 1927

fell before the storm passed. Rivers and creeks overflowed their banks. Downtown Montpelier was under 8 to 10 feet (2.4 to 3 meters) of water.

The Flood of 1927 was Vermont's deadliest natural disaster. The flood killed 84 people, including Lieutenant Governor S. Hollister Jackson. The flood destroyed bridges, roads, railroads, homes, and businesses.

The Flood of 1927 changed many things in Vermont. Many railroads were not rebuilt. Instead, the state paved existing roads and built new highways. To prevent future floods, the government built dams and reservoirs on the Winooski River in East Orange, Wrightsville, and Waterbury.

Depression and World War II

In 1929, the U.S. stock market crashed. The crash was the start of the Great Depression (1929–1939). Throughout the United States, many companies went out of business. Millions of people were left without jobs.

In Vermont, the Great Depression added to the state's hard times. In 1932, the U.S. government started programs to help workers who had lost their jobs. Vermonters built ski trails, schools, and dams in the state.

In 1941, the United States entered World War II (1939–1945). About 38,000 Vermont soldiers helped the United States and its allies win the war.

Recent Years

After World War II, business and industry increased in the state. In 1957, International Business Machines (IBM) opened a factory in Essex Junction. Today, IBM is Vermont's largest employer. About 8,000 Vermonters work for IBM.

By the 1960s, interstate highways connected Vermont with Massachusetts and Canada. The highways brought many people to the state. Low crime rates, clean air, and strong school systems attracted new residents. The state also became popular with tourists.

Vermonters believe in protecting their state's land, water, air, and scenery. In 1968, the General Assembly passed a law that banned billboards. Besides Vermont, only Maine, Alaska, and Hawaii do not allow billboards. Two years later, the General Assembly passed Act 250. This law includes strict rules for building businesses and houses in the state.

In 2000, Vermont received national attention. The state passed the country's first law that allowed same-sex couples to form a legal relationship. These relationships include many of the rights granted to married couples.

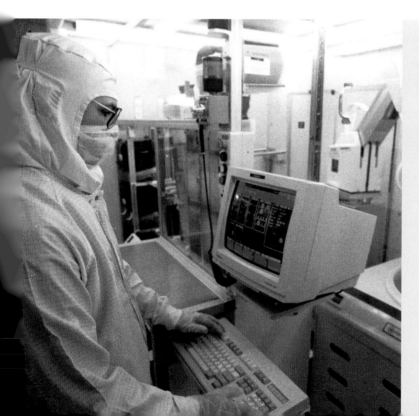

Workers at IBM's factory in Essex Junction produce and test computer microchips. The workers' protective clothing helps keep the microchips free from dust and dirt.

The current capitol, called the State House, was built in Montpelier in 1859.

Chapter 4

Government and Politics

Vermonters are known for their independence. The Green Mountain Boys fought for independence from New York and New Hampshire in the early 1770s. They fought again for independence from Great Britain during the Revolutionary War. Vermont was an independent republic from 1777 to 1791. Over the years, many Vermont politicians and voters have called themselves "independents." In 2003, Vermont's only U.S. representative and one of its U.S. senators were independents.

State Government

Vermont's government is divided into three branches. They are the legislative, executive, and judicial branches.

The legislative branch makes the state's laws. Vermont's legislature is often called the General Assembly. The General Assembly includes 30 state senators and 150 state representatives. Assembly members serve two-year terms.

The executive branch makes sure people follow the state's laws. The governor leads the executive branch. Until 1870, Vermonters elected a new governor each year. Governors now are elected every two years. New Hampshire is the only other state where governors serve two-year terms.

Five elected officials work with the governor. These officials are the lieutenant governor, the secretary of state, the state treasurer, the attorney general, and the state auditor. They each serve two-year terms.

Vermont Courts

The judicial branch makes decisions about Vermont laws. The branch includes several courts. Each court makes decisions on different types of cases. Criminal cases are tried in district courts. Superior courts mainly hear cases that do not involve crimes. Family courts, probate courts, traffic courts, and municipal courts are other types of Vermont courts. The state

Vermont's State Government

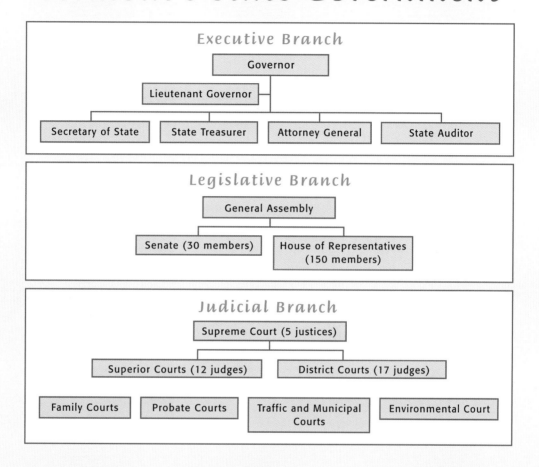

Executive Branch

- Governor
- Lieutenant Governor
- Secretary of State
- State Treasurer
- Attorney General
- State Auditor

Legislative Branch

- General Assembly
  - Senate (30 members)
  - House of Representatives (150 members)

Judicial Branch

- Supreme Court (5 justices)
  - Superior Courts (12 judges)
  - District Courts (17 judges)
- Family Courts
- Probate Courts
- Traffic and Municipal Courts
- Environmental Court

also has an environmental court that hears cases that deal with the environment and zoning laws.

The supreme court is Vermont's highest court. People who do not agree with the decisions of lower courts can take cases to the supreme court. This court makes the final decision on court cases in Vermont.

Calvin Coolidge

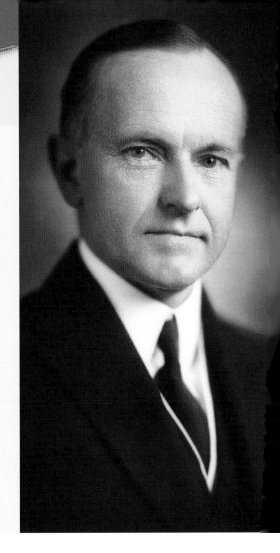

Calvin Coolidge is the only president who was born on July 4. He was born in Plymouth, Vermont, in 1872. He later moved to Massachusetts. In 1918, he was elected governor of Massachusetts. Two years later, he became vice president under Republican President Warren Harding. When Harding died in office in 1923, Coolidge became the 30th president. He was sworn in as president while visiting his father in Vermont.

In 1924, Coolidge was elected to the presidency. During his term, the U.S. economy had one of its strongest periods in history. Coolidge served until 1929. He died January 5, 1933.

The Republican Party

For many years, Vermont voters supported the Republican party. In 1854, Vermont elected its first Republican governor, Stephen Royce. The state did not have a Democratic governor until Philip Hoff was elected in 1962. The state elected its first Democratic U.S. senator, Patrick Leahy, in 1974. He was elected again in 1980, 1986, 1992, and 1998.

One of the most important Republicans of the 20th century was George Aiken. He served Vermont as a state senator and lieutenant governor before being elected governor in 1936. Aiken served two terms as governor before being elected to the U.S. Senate in 1940.

Aiken worked to improve life for Vermonters and other rural Americans. He worked with the Rural Electrification Administration (REA) to bring electricity to farm families. In 1964, Aiken helped start the nation's food stamp program. This program helps people with low incomes pay for food. Aiken retired from the Senate in 1975 and died in 1984.

Recent Government Events

In 2001, one of Vermont's U.S. senators left the Republican party to become independent. Jim Jeffords' decision had a major effect on U.S. politics. The balance of power in the U.S. Senate shifted from the Republicans to the Democrats.

Vermont's constitution requires that elected officials receive at least 50 percent of the total votes cast. If no candidate receives 50 percent of the votes, the General Assembly chooses the winner. In 2002, the Republican candidate for governor, James Douglas, received 45 percent of votes. Democrat Doug Racine received 42 percent. Assembly members voted 159 to 16 to elect James Douglas governor.

Ben Cohen (left) and Jerry Greenfield (right) sold their ice cream company in 2000 for $326 million.

Chapter 5

Economy and Resources

Vermont is famous for businesses that start small and grow into large companies. In 1978, Ben Cohen and Jerry Greenfield started making ice cream in an old gas station in Burlington. Today, Ben and Jerry's Homemade produces nearly 20 million gallons (76 million liters) of ice cream each year at its factories in Waterbury, St. Albans, and Springfield.

In 1981, John Sortino began making teddy bears in his home in Burlington. The Vermont Teddy Bear Company now makes about 350,000 teddy bears each year at factories in Shelburne and Newport. The company ships the bears to people all over the world.

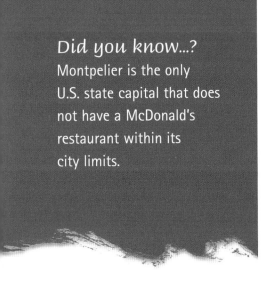

Service Industries

Service industries provide the largest number of jobs and amount of income in Vermont. Resorts, stores, banks, and government agencies are all examples of Vermont service businesses.

Tourism is Vermont's top service industry. About 12 million people visit Vermont each year. More than 34,000 Vermonters work in tourism jobs.

Skiing is the state's top tourist activity. More than 20 alpine ski resorts and 50 cross-country ski areas provide jobs for about 13,000 people. Mountains near Stowe and Killington are among Vermont's most popular skiing and snowboarding areas.

During fall, many tourists come to Vermont to see the brightly colored leaves. Vermonters sometimes call these visitors "leaf peepers."

Manufacturing

Manufacturing is the second largest industry in Vermont. The area near Burlington was once famous for its woolen mills. By 1950, most mills had moved to southern states.

Skiers enjoy a day of downhill skiing at Sugarbush Resort in Warren.

41

Today, Vermont's largest factories produce electrical equipment and electronic parts. Other factories produce machinery, metal parts, and machine tools.

Vermont is home to one of the world's largest snowboard companies. In 1977, Jake Burton Carpenter began making snowboards in Londonderry. Today, Burton Snowboards makes about one-third of the snowboards sold in the United States at its Burlington factory.

Agriculture

Agriculture has been important in Vermont throughout the state's history. Dairy farming has been especially important. Each year, Vermont produces about 2.7 billion pounds (1.2 billion kilograms) of milk and more than 100 million pounds (45 million kilograms) of cheese. Vermont farmers also raise beef cattle, sheep, and hogs.

Holstein dairy cattle roam in a farm pasture near Sutton.

Vermont produces other farm products. The state is the largest producer of maple syrup in the United States. Farmers also grow apples, hay, vegetables, greenhouse plants, and Christmas trees.

Mining

People first mined Vermont's large stone deposits in the late 1700s. Mining is still important in the state. The Rock of Ages quarry in Barre is one of the largest monumental granite quarries in the world. Much of this quarry's gray stone is carved into gravestones. The granite was also used to build the State House in Montpelier.

The Rutland and Proctor area is home to high-quality marble. Vermont marble was used to build both the Jefferson Memorial and the Supreme Court Building in Washington, D.C.

Slate is also mined in Vermont. Most of Vermont's slate is mined in the Slate Valley near Fair Haven. The slate is used for floors, fireplaces, kitchen countertops, and roofs.

Maple Syrup

Each year, Vermont produces about 275 million gallons (1 billion liters) of maple syrup. This amount is nearly 40 percent of the nation's maple syrup.

The maple trees' sap runs when nights are cold and days are warm. The maple sugar season begins in late February and lasts until April.

To collect maple sap, people push devices called taps into maple tree trunks. The sap drips out into buckets. Millions of maple trees are tapped each spring during the harvest. The sap is boiled in buildings called sugarhouses. To get 1 gallon (4 liters) of maple syrup, producers must boil about 40 gallons (151 liters) of sap.

Logging

Vermont's thick forests have been an important resource for the state since its early days. The trees are used in construction and to make furniture, paper, and pulp products.

Vermont's government wants to protect its forests. It has passed laws that control how and where loggers can harvest trees. Some loggers say the laws have forced them out of the logging business.

BREAKFAST

WOODSTOCK
PHARMACY
Founded 1853

n. t. ferro
custom jewelers
est. 1947

Founded in 1761, the historic town of Woodstock is popular with tourists.

Chapter 6

People and Culture

With 608,827 people, Vermont has the second smallest state population. Only Wyoming has fewer people.

Vermont is a rural state. About 70 percent of Vermonters live in rural areas or towns of less than 2,500 people. The largest city, Burlington, has only about 40,000 people. With about 8,000 people, Montpelier is the smallest U.S. state capital.

Located in the central part of the state, Woodstock has been called the prettiest small town in America. The townspeople work hard to keep the town's historic look. No utility wires appear overhead. Instead, the wires are buried in the ground to keep them out of sight.

Did you know...?
Before 1965, each town in Vermont had its own representative in the General Assembly. The smallest town had the same voting power as the largest city. In 1962, the U.S. Supreme Court ordered the Vermont House of Representatives to base representation on population. Three years later, the house reduced its size from 246 members to 150.

Ethnic Groups

Most of the first Vermont settlers came from other New England states and New York. Most of these people had English or French backgrounds. In the mid-1800s, many Italians moved to Vermont to work in the stone quarries. Barre still has a large Italian population.

Most Vermonters are white. Only about 3,000 Vermonters are African American. Burlington has the state's largest Hispanic and Asian populations.

Vermont had a large American Indian population before European settlers came. Today, only about 2,400 Indians live in Vermont. Most of them belong to the Abenaki tribe.

Festivals and Fairs

Vermont celebrates its heritage and its people in a number of festivals held around the state. Maple Open House Weekend takes place during sugaring season. Sugarhouses around the

Vermont's Ethnic Backgrounds

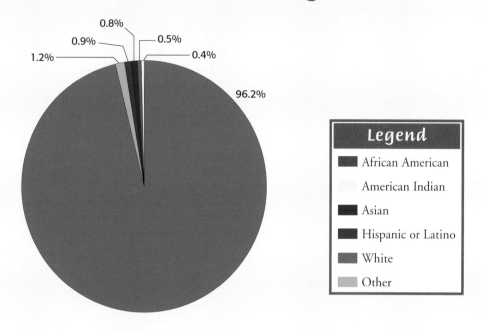

0.8%

0.9%

0.5%

1.2%

0.4%

96.2%

Legend

African American

American Indian

Asian

Hispanic or Latino

White

Other

state invite visitors to see how maple syrup is made. Each April, people come to St. Albans for the Vermont Maple Festival. The festival includes maple sugaring demonstrations, a pancake breakfast, and a talent show. In June, people visit Brattleboro for the Strolling of the Heifers. People march 30 young cows up the town's main street as part of this festival.

Many Vermont county fairs and town festivals celebrate farming. The biggest event is the Vermont State Fair, held each year in Rutland. The 10-day event features concerts, a demolition derby, horse-pulling events, and a farm museum.

Other Vermont events honor the arts. Each Memorial Day weekend, artists around the state open their studios to visitors. This event is called Open Studio Weekend. The Art on the Mountain festival has been held in Wilmington since 1963. During the 16-day event, visitors can see the work of glassblowers, quilters, painters, potters, and other Vermont artists.

Outdoor Fun

Vermont's mountains, forests, and lakes offer many opportunities for outdoor fun. Skiing, snowboarding, hiking, fishing, and boating are some of the activities both Vermonters and visitors enjoy.

Vermont has many ski resorts. One of the best known is the Trapp Family Lodge in Stowe. Georg and Maria von Trapp and their children settled in Vermont in 1939. The popular play and movie *The Sound of Music* is based on the

The Trapp Family Lodge near Stowe includes more than 2,700 acres (1,093 hectares) of land. Lodge visitors enjoy skiing and snowshoeing in winter and hiking and mountain biking in summer.

"I shall always write about the country. I suppose I show a sad side to it too often. It only seems sad to those who love the city."
—Robert Frost, poet and longtime Vermont resident

family's story. Today, members of the von Trapp family still run the lodge.

Artists, Writers, and Musicians

A number of well-known writers have ties to Vermont. Poet Robert Frost was born in California, but he spent his later years in Vermont. His many famous poems include "The Road Not Taken." Writer Dorothy Canfield Fisher lived in Arlington until she died in the late 1950s. She wrote the children's book *Understood Betsy*. Sinclair Lewis was born in Minnesota and later lived in Barnard. His book *It Can't Happen Here* takes place in Vermont.

Well-known artists and musicians also have Vermont roots. Artist Norman Rockwell painted some of his most famous *Saturday Evening Post* covers while living in Arlington in the 1930s and 1940s. The popular rock band Phish formed at the University of Vermont in 1983.

Covered Bridges

The Batten Kill River Bridge in West Arlington, at left, is one of more than 100 covered bridges in Vermont. This number is the largest of any state.

The bridges' roofs protect the wooden trusses that support the bridges. If the trusses are exposed to harsh weather, they would only last about 10 years. With roofs, the trusses last much longer.

Some of Vermont's covered bridges are nearly 200 years old. The state's oldest covered bridge is Pulp Mill Bridge on Otter Creek. This bridge was built between 1808 and 1820. The nation's longest covered bridge connects Windsor, Vermont, and Cornish, New Hampshire. The Cornish-Windsor Bridge is 449 feet (137 meters) long.

Vermont's Future

Today, Vermont's leaders struggle with many issues. Like many other states that rely on tourism, Vermont is concerned with its environment. Water safety, energy sources, and transportation are all important issues. But with a low crime rate and a strong educational system, Vermont continues to be a state with much to offer.

Recipe: Maple Squares

Vermont's thick forests of maple trees produce more maple syrup than those in any other state. Maple syrup gives these easy-to-make squares their sweet flavor.

Ingredients

¾ cup (175 mL) peanut butter
½ cup (120 mL) maple syrup
1½ cups (360 mL) nonfat dry
  milk powder
2 tablespoons (30 mL) chopped
  peanuts

Equipment

medium mixing bowl
dry-ingredient measuring
  cups
liquid measuring cup
mixing spoon
9-inch by 13-inch
  (23-centimeter by
  33-centimeter)
  baking pan
rubber spatula
measuring spoons
kitchen knife

What you do

1. In medium bowl, mix the peanut butter and maple syrup with mixing spoon until well blended.

2. Add milk powder to peanut butter mixture and stir well.

3. Spread the mixture into baking pan with rubber spatula.

4. Pat mixture down to make an even layer.

5. Sprinkle the peanuts over the mixture and press gently.

6. Chill 1 hour.

7. Cut into 1-inch (2.5-centimeter) squares. Keep covered and chilled until serving.

Makes 32 squares

Vermont's Flag and Seal

Vermont's Flag

The current Vermont flag was adopted in 1919. The flag has a blue background with the state coat of arms in the middle. The coat of arms is similar to the state seal, except it is shaped like a shield. Pine boughs wrap around the shield. A deer's head at the top of the shield stands for Vermont's wildlife. A red banner at the bottom of the shield reads "Vermont, Freedom and Unity."

Vermont's State Seal

Vermont adopted its state seal in 1937. The seal includes a pine tree, a spear, a cow, and four sheaves of wheat. Wooded hills represent the Green Mountains. Wavy lines at the top and bottom of the seal stand for water and sky. The words "Vermont" and the state motto, "Freedom and Unity," are at the bottom of the seal.

Almanac

Nickname: Green Mountain State

Population: 608,827 (U.S. Census, 2000)
Population rank: 49th

Capital: Montpelier

Largest communities: Burlington, Essex, Rutland, South Burlington, Barre

Agricultural products: Dairy products, greenhouse plants, hay, vegetables, maple syrup

Agriculture

Area: 9,249 square miles (23,955 square kilometers)
Size rank: 43rd

Highest point: Mount Mansfield, 4,393 feet (1,339 meters)

Lowest point: Lake Champlain, 95 feet (29 meters)

Geography

Average summer temperature: 65 degrees Fahrenheit (18 degrees Celsius)

Average winter temperature: 18 degrees Fahrenheit (minus 8 degrees Celsius)

Average annual precipitation: 40 inches (102 centimeters)

Climate

Red clover

56

Hermit thrush

Animal: Morgan horse

Bird: Hermit thrush

Butterfly: Monarch

Flower: Red clover

Insect: Honeybee

Economy

Natural resources: Timber, granite, marble, slate, crushed stone, gravel, talc, and gemstones

Types of industry: Manufacture of machine tools, furniture, and computer parts; food processing; logging; mining

Symbols

Rocks: Granite, marble, and slate

Song: "These Green Mountains" by Diane Martin

Tree: Sugar maple

Government

First governor: Thomas Chittendon, 1791–1797

Statehood: March 4, 1791; 14th state

U.S. Representatives: 1

U.S. Senators: 2

U.S. electoral votes: 3

Counties: 14

Timeline

State History

1000
Abenaki and Mahican people are living in Vermont.

1609
French explorer Samuel de Champlain sails into Lake Champlain.

1749
Vermont becomes known as the New Hampshire Grants.

1777
Vermont becomes an independent republic.

1791
Vermont becomes the 14th state on March 4.

1816
An Indonesian volcano that erupted in 1815 causes the "year without a summer."

1881
Vermonter Chester Arthur becomes president of the United States.

U.S. History

1620
Pilgrims establish a colony in the New World.

1754–1763
Great Britain and France fight the French and Indian War.

1775–1783
American colonists fight the British during the Revolutionary War.

1812–1814
The United States and Great Britain fight the War of 1812.

1861–1865
The Union and the Confederacy fight the Civil War.

1927
A huge flood kills 84 people in Vermont.

1923
Vermont native Calvin Coolidge becomes president of the United States.

1957
IBM opens a plant in Essex Junction.

1968
Vermont bans billboards.

2001
Senator Jim Jeffords leaves the Republican Party; Senate power switches to the Democrats.

1929–1939
Many Americans lose jobs during the Great Depression.

1964
U.S. Congress passes the Civil Rights Act, which makes discrimination illegal.

1914–1918
World War I is fought; the United States enters the war in 1917.

1939–1945
World War II is fought; the United States enters the war in 1941.

2001
On September 11, terrorists attack the World Trade Center and the Pentagon.

Words to Know

canal (kuh-NAL)—a channel dug across land to connect two bodies of water

glacier (GLAY-shur)—a large, slow-moving sheet of ice and snow

granite (GRAN-it)—a hard, gray rock used in the construction of buildings

independent (in-di-PEN-duhnt)—free from the control of other people or things

quarry (KWOR-ee)—a place where stones are dug or cut from the ground

republic (ree-PUHB-lik)—a government headed by a president with officials elected by voters

textile (TEK-stile)—a fabric or cloth that has been woven or knitted

tourism (TOOR-iz-um)—the business of providing entertainment, food, and lodging for travelers

truss (TRUHSS)—a beam that supports the structure of a bridge

To Learn More

Doak, Robin S. *Calvin Coolidge.* Profiles of the Presidents. Minneapolis: Compass Point Books, 2003.

Foran, Jill. *Vermont.* A Guide to American States. Mankato, Minn.: Weigl Publishers, 2001.

Heinrichs, Ann. *Vermont.* America the Beautiful. New York: Children's Press, 2001.

Raabe, Emily. *Ethan Allen: The Green Mountain Boys and Vermont's Path to Statehood.* The Library of American Lives and Times. New York: PowerPlus Books, 2002.

Internet Sites

Do you want to find out more about Vermont?
Let FactHound, our fact-finding hound dog, do the research for you.

Here's how:
1) Visit *http://www.facthound.com*
2) Type in the Book ID number:
   0736822011
3) Click on FETCH IT.

FactHound will fetch Internet sites picked by our editors just for you!

Places to Write and Visit

Ben and Jerry's Ice Cream Factory
Route 100
Waterbury, VT 05676

Bennington Battle Monument
15 Monument Circle
Old Bennington, VT 05201

Ethan Allen Homestead and Museum
1 Ethan Allen Homestead, Suite 2
Burlington, VT 05401

Green Mountain National Forest
231 North Main Street
Rutland, VT 05701

President Calvin Coolidge State Historic Site
Vermont Highway 100A, P.O. Box 247
Plymouth, VT 05056

Vermont Department of Tourism and Marketing
6 Baldwin Street, Drawer 33
Montpelier, VT 05633-1301

Vermont Marble Museum
52 Main Street, P.O. Box 607
Proctor, VT 05765